INTRODUCTION BY ROBERT ELMAN

A WORLD OF ANIMALS BY RIEN POORTVLIET

The Living Forest

HARRY N. ABRAMS, INC., PUBLISHERS
NEW YORK

PEACOCK PRESS/BANTAM BOOKS
NEW YORK, LONDON, TORONTO

Translated from the Dutch by Marlies Comjean

LIBRARY OF CONGRESS CATALOGING IN PUBLICATION DATA

Poortvliet, Rien.
The living forest: a world of animals.
Translation of De vossen hebben holen.
1. Animals, Habits and behavior of—Pictorial works.
2. Birds—Behavior—Pictorial works. I. Title.
QL751.P5413   599   79-11424

Library of Congress Catalog Card Number: 79-11424

Originally published under the title *De Vossen Hebben Holen*
© 1973 Unieboek BV-Van Holkema & Warendorf, Bussum
English translation © 1979 Harry N. Abrams, Inc.

Harry N. Abrams, Inc. Edition: ISBN 0-8109-0911-1
Peacock Press/Bantam Books Edition: ISBN 0-553-01237-1

Printed and bound in the United States

Introduction

It is no mere coincidence that many notable painters have also been eminent naturalists. Such artists as Alexander Wilson, John James Audubon, Ernest Thompson Seton, Louis Agassiz Fuertes, Roger Tory Peterson—to cite a few chosen at random—might never have succeeded so well in penetrating and interpreting nature's labyrinths had they lacked the painter's strengths: sharpness of observation, insatiable curiosity, limitless patience in studying each subject, an absolute greed for detail, and a mind both creative and pragmatic. A mind unwilling to formulate theories of biology or animal behavior without evidence but willing to accept even the fantastic when the observed evidence warrants acceptance.

These are the strengths that flavor the work of Rien Poortvliet, Holland's most popular illustrator. He is well known and loved there—and indeed is earning increasing respect in America and elsewhere—for the charming, imaginative aspects of his work as well as for his skill and interpretive insight. It is not just Poortvliet's drawings that have caught the fancy of his readers. The man himself has many admirers, drawn to him by the same appealing qualities that mark his work. In this respect, Poortvliet has been compared to Norman Rockwell, the much-adored rural American painter. Like Rockwell, Poortvliet is unspoiled by success and has never courted popularity nor shown a trace of arrogance about his fame.

Poortvliet is an avid naturalist who lives in a rustic cottage with his family on the edge of the woods. He spends much time afield, gaining an intensely intimate acquaintance with the wild denizens of the forest, the fields, and Holland's marshy polders. Here, Poortvliet is not an intruder but an observer—at times, perhaps, becoming as much a part of the woods as the animals he paints.

Drawing has long been a passion for Poortvliet, and even as a boy he dreamed of going to art school. His parents, however, had other ideas, and wanted a more "down-to-earth" profession for their son. So Poortvliet became an advertising executive, and for fifteen years he drew "happy families eating t.v. dinners," while illustrating books in his spare time. Eight years ago, he decided to do full time what pleased him most—illustrating books.

Poortvliet's first few books have enjoyed a huge success in Holland, Denmark, and West Germany. His subjects are by no means limited to wild animals. He has illustrated such books as *The Small Dutch Farm*, *Hunting*, *Horses*, *Horses* (Poortvliet was invited to sketch the thoroughbreds in Queen Elizabeth's stables), and a singular religious book, *He Was One of Us*, which is a sensitive re-creation of the life of Jesus of Nazareth. He became known on this side of the Atlantic with the appearance in English of *Gnomes*, a phenomenal bestseller on which he collaborated with a scientist friend, Wil Huygen.

As in *Gnomes*, Poortvliet's work in *The Living Forest* is a glorious celebration of nature. Again he reveals his enduring fascination for the natural world around him in his own unique style of scientific exactitude, wit, and imagination. Bearded and pipe-smoking, Poortvliet is an individualist who paints what he chooses in the way he chooses, according to no one's standards but his own. He is devoted to his work, spending almost seven days a week painting, sketching, and drawing. Poortvliet shows the fragile beauty of nature but does not shy away from nature's brutalities; we see the realities—often harsh—of life in and out of the forest. At times we get a glimpse of an earthy side to his character, as in the illustration depicting a Dutch farm girl from a rather unconventional angle—looking up her skirt.

Poortvliet's art reveals certain contradictions—and many strengths. His style is realistic and highly factual, yet it has a loose immediacy and spontaneity achieved not by studying mounted specimens for anatomically perfect but stilted drawings, but by actually going into the field for his models. While depicting animals and their habitats with incredible accuracy, he captures them in a lively and almost impressionistic way.

Another, perhaps unexpected, quality has enormous value for the artist-naturalist: the quality of wit. The very act of painting requires great self-assurance, yet the interpreter of nature must not take himself, his discipline, or his peers so seriously as to lose perspective. If he does, nature—to say nothing of his colleagues and critics—will mock him. Poortvliet sees, and shows what he sees, with humility and wit.

Poortvliet relishes nature's quirks and shares them with us. He calls our attention to the fact that the fox, its intelligence notwithstanding, is really more timid than shy; that the hen pheasant, a doting but flighty mother, has trouble counting her chicks; that the wild piglet's nursery pelage is a coat of protective coloration but looks to the human observer like striped pajamas; that the wild boar is such a brutal lover as to provoke screams from a protesting sow; that the rabbit, having evolved nervous responses too taut for decisiveness, is often pitiably torn between crouching and running; that the tines of a deer's antlers inflict injury less often than they prevent it; and that the mallard drake is an incorrigible lecher, eager to force his advances on any female of his own kind and even on domestic ducks, thus fathering some bizarre offspring.

To a reader unfamiliar with nature's ways, a few of Poortvliet's more startling observations may seem almost incredible—but they are quite accurate. Scientists have long pondered the evolution of the mallard drake's lechery and carelessness in the choice of mates, for instance. In 1843, Audubon examined a duck unlike any he had ever seen. He listed it as a new species, which he named the Brewer's duck in tribute to Thomas Brewer, an ornithologist he admired. But field naturalists even then knew about the frequency of hybridization among ducks, and in describing his new species Audubon admitted that it might be a cross between the mallard and "some other species, perhaps the Gadwall, to which also it bears a good resemblance." Such circumspection was well founded. The Brewer's duck proved to be a mallard-gadwall—or madwall or gadard, if you prefer.

Many ducks hybridize rather freely, though the mallard seems to be unsurpassed in that regard. Waterfowl can see colors, and what prevents them from courting mates of the wrong species is recognition of combined factors: color, size, specific courting behavior, and habitat preferences. Yet ducks do occasionally interbreed and produce hybrid young. Such offspring are sometimes infertile, sometimes unwanted as mates, and sometimes shy of other ducks—uninterested in mating. Otherwise, all of those duck species that share the same general habitat, habits, and food requirements might eventually be blended into one drab duck, a kind of uniduck. Nature's ways are, indeed, intriguing. With her safeguards against an ultimate blending, she maintains the diversity that marks a healthy ecosystem. (Diversity is itself an important safeguard in nature; a plague or parasite or predator that devastates one species may be harmless to another and, moreover, the many forms of life depend on one another for sustenance and various services and even as "buffers" between themselves and various enemies.)

Poortvliet understands this well, and although his chapter on ducks focuses on the mallard, he also portrays the shoveler, the pintail, eider, teal, and widgeon—other species that inhabit both North America and Europe—as well as several strictly Eurasian varieties. He depicts swans and geese, too, and some of the interactions among the various types of waterfowl. And he does not befog fact with fable or sensitivity with sentimentality; he takes care to mention that swans kill ducklings.

A difficulty with many popularizers of nature—particularly with regard to animal behavior and habits— is the tendency to impose the value judgments of human society on wildlife. A swan is not "noble" in the moral sense because it is beautiful, nor is it a villain because it must compete mercilessly with ducks in order to survive. A fox is not "crafty" because it is instinctively cautious and has the ability to learn both evasive and acquisitive tactics that let it, too, survive. Even a naturalist as eminent as Ernest Thompson Seton once let himself be dazzled by suppositions of that kind in a book called *Wild Animals I Have Known.* John Burroughs quipped that Seton should have titled it *Wild Animals I Alone Have Known.* Poortvliet avoids the anthropomorphic trap, evoking empathy without losing his objectivity.

For American readers, that empathy will be strengthened by a sense of recognition—of some familiarity with most of the wild creatures depicted. For although Poortvliet describes those animals that are his particular favorites in his own woods and fields, his subjects are not exclusively Dutch, nor even exclusively European in most cases. In fact, readers may be pleasantly startled to encounter here a few species they had regarded as purely American. They may be surprised to see the badger—a creature they had assumed was native only to lower Canada and the United States. Or they may be puzzled at first to see what looks like a portrait of a Rocky Mountain elk with a caption labeling it a red deer.

Some biologists once classified the European red deer and the elk as two regional representatives, or subspecies, of a single species. Most now label the European and American animals as distinct though closely related species. Anyone who has seen both animals may have difficulty in accepting the notion that they are brothers under the skin, for the elk is so big that its skin might hold almost a red deer and a half. But size is sometimes a poor criterion for differentiating between species. Many years ago, some Rocky Mountain elk were transplanted to a large, mountainous preserve in New England. Over the succeeding generations, they have adapted to their new habitat through a reduction in body mass. These elk, like most European red deer, are now about the size of a big mule deer. And so, one observer's bull elk is another observer's red stag. Additional varieties—species or subspecies—of red deer inhabit Asia. Part of Poortvliet's charm lies in rediscovering the familiar in an exotic setting, as well as the exotic in some surprisingly familiar settings.

The principal players in this book are the red fox, roe deer, black grouse, wild boar, mallard, hare and rabbit, red deer and fallow deer, pheasant, gray partridge, and mouflon. Other species appear occasionally in the paintings or text, but these are the starring characters. Together they form a cosmopolitan cast.

The red fox hunts for birds and rodents through Europe, in northeastern Africa, over Asia, and as far south as central Europe. Until fairly recently, the red fox of the New World was believed to have been a distinct species that interbred with European foxes long ago imported to America by colonial sportsmen who yearned to ride to the hounds. At that time, the American red fox was known in Canada but no farther south than New England, for the expansion of its range was blocked by enormous hardwood forests— an adequate environment for America's gray fox but unsuitable habitat for the red fox.

The spread of the latter species over great portions of North America was less a result of importation or interbreeding (though both occurred) than of man's impact on the environment. Some readers may be perplexed by Poortvliet's statement that the red fox is native to both the Old World and the New and that the dozen American varieties belong to the same species as the European fox, but Poortvliet is quite right. The fox is as widely distributed as that very different group of magnificently antlered creatures—some of them unique in anatomical detail but all closely related to one another—known regionally as wapiti, elk, red deer, hangul, shou, or Persian maral.

The mallard, too, has an almost worldwide distribution, as have several other species of waterfowl. Among the upland birds, the ringnecked pheasant has the widest distribution, thanks to man's fondness for it as a source of food, a game bird, and a symbol of natural beauty. It originated neither in Europe nor in America but in Asia.

Poortvliet is of course careful to point out differences as well as similarities among the creatures of the New and Old Worlds. Hares and rabbits, for example, are familiar in both Europe and America, and superficially they look pretty much alike. But the most common hares are of different varieties, and so are the rabbits (except transplanted European populations). Oddly, America's rabbits—more than a dozen species and nearly seventy subspecies of cottontails—in some respects behave more like hares than rabbits. They rest in forms like hares and dig no warrens, as European rabbits do, although they will use the burrows of other animals to escape cold or predators.

Among Poortvliet's other starring characters, most have become established in America in large numbers (the gray, or Hungarian, partridge; the wild boar) or have at least been imported in small numbers (the fallow deer, the roe deer). Only the black grouse and the mouflon are virtually unknown on this side of the Atlantic. And even the pictures and descriptions of these two creatures may arouse a feeling of vague recognition, of something almost remembered. In the case of the mouflon, the reason may be fairly obvious: the relationship with American wild sheep such as the bighorn and, for that matter, with domestic sheep, which are thought to be descended from two or three wild varieties—the mouflon, the Asian urial, and possibly the Asian argali. Poortvliet's mouflon portrait also reveals physical similarities to North America's wild Dall and Stone sheep.

As to the black grouse, that European bird is closely related to varieties of grouse and ptarmigan found in North America and has some resemblance to America's spruce grouse, though the spruce grouse is smaller, has only scattered black in its plumage, and wears much smaller scarlet combs over its eyes.

Even among the minor, or supporting, characters in this book, a North American reader may feel an enjoyable if mystifying sense of previous encounter. The barnacle goose (so named because it was once believed to hatch from barnacles) bears a resemblance to the Eastern brant. Europe's most common wild goose, the graylag, is the chief progenitor of domestic geese. It somewhat resembles and is related to a couple of wild American varieties.

These close relationships and similarities—as well as differences—are not always so apparent in books about wild creatures in distant lands. Nor do those creatures always seem so alive in book illustrations. What makes them so recognizable and alive in Poortvliet's work is his true understanding of his subjects, which allows him to render nature's richness of detail, expression, and dynamism.

Robert Elman
Greentown, Pennsylvania

You will already have noticed, leafing through this book, that it is full of drawings of animals who live in the wild. It is intended to let you *see* clearly what they look like, how they live.

Because I am often on watch outdoors, I can observe wild animals in a leisurely way, and I learn a great deal—as you do from firsthand observation. In our schools we hear much talk about animals, but mostly in a chewed-over, bookish fashion that does not really tell you very much. If you want to know an animal better, you have to find out more about it than you can by looking at it just once: you have to watch how it moves, eats, sleeps—in short, how it lives. Of course, there are many animal books that describe wildlife, among them well-known field guides. But I have noticed that such publications devote as much space to a fox, for example, as to a mouse! I *do* find that strange! Wouldn't anyone be more thrilled to see a fox than a mouse? In this book, therefore, you will mainly find those animals that are most appealing: "Brother Fox," "Brother Deer," "Mrs. Duck," and many others who share the land with us.

With each of my drawings I wanted to say something special; therefore, there is a short introduction for each kind of animal, and some brief notes next to the pictures.

In the Bible (St. Luke 9:58) Jesus says: "Foxes have holes, and birds of the air have nests . . ."

Thus, every creature has its own kind of shelter—the fox a hole, the bird a nest, the wild boar a lair, and the rabbit a burrow.

Just as it is written in Genesis: "And God made the beasts of the earth according to their kind . . ."

Rien Poortvliet
Soestdunen

The Fox

Hardly any animal is as appealing as the fox. A male is about a yard long, including his tail. An especially beautiful animal, a jewel! Particularly in his thick winter coat, orange red, with white bands, a white tip to his tail, smart black ears, and black "boots." And in addition to that—probably most distinctive—his unusually slim snout! Hence his popularity, his proverbial sharpness: "As sly as a fox"; "When the fox preaches, farmer, watch your chickens"; "Reynard is still Reynard though he put on a cowl."

Is he then so sly, so cunning? Well, much as it may seem so, Reynard is really just terribly cautious and suspicious! When he smells or hears something that could be a tidbit for him, he does not rush right up to it, but makes a wide circle around it first. You would think only a small snake could hide in that grass! Yet the fox moves so carefully that he almost always outsmarts the hunter.

In suburban areas, and even in some densely settled agricultural regions, few people ever catch sight of a fox. There are regions where many people assume that he is practically extinct. But that is not the case. Generally speaking, the number of foxes increases all the time, and the animal is adaptable enough to multiply even when living close to man. Various subspecies, or regional races, of the common red fox are found in Europe, North America, Asia, and Africa. In North America alone, there are a dozen subspecies of red fox (plus the gray fox and several other species). In parts of the United States and in some European countries—Holland, for example—biologists working for government agencies estimate that there are too many red foxes for the good of various prey species, including many types of birds. On the other hand, the foxes help to control the populations of rodents.

Brother Fox usually stays in hiding during the day, but when it gets darker, he sneaks from cover to cover, through trenches and dry ditches. The fox has to hunt carefully, using ears, nose, and eyes, while the prey, the rabbit, can hop around happily all across the meadow—the grass is not going to run away.

In the spring, when there is plenty of food for foxes—young rabbits and hares, small rodents, and the eggs of ground breeders such as pheasants, partridges, and woodcock—four to seven young foxes are born deep down in the den. The parents drag in quite a bit of food, usually more than enough, playing havoc with small creatures. At birth young foxes are no bigger than moles, grayish in color, and blind. They grow like cabbages and when they get a little bigger, the mother allows them to play outside from time to time. After four or five months they are on their own.

You might think it interesting to raise a fox pup as a pet. Unfortunately, it does not work! I speak from experience. As long as the foxes are quite small it is all right, but when they grow up they become timid and distrustful. A fox is just not a dog. Dogs originally lived in groups and know how to obey a "leader." For a dog, his master is the "top dog" and he likes that. But a fox lives alone and does not become attached to anyone. No, even if you find one, you will spare yourself and the pup a lot of misery if you leave the small animal where it belongs: free in the wild. That is what the fox likes best—where the fox is at his best!

In North America, the fox population was at one time depleted by unregulated trapping for the fur trade, coupled with campaigns of extermination by poultry farmers. Throughout most of the animal's range in the United States, the red fox is now regarded as a game animal or valuable furbearer. Its population is watched and controlled by state conservation agencies, so that the species will neither decline nor become overabundant.

I see so little of my red friend, unfortunately —
I really try my best, but I see him seldom...

oh well, that is the way the fox likes it!

Yet as soon as it gets quiet and dusky, he appears

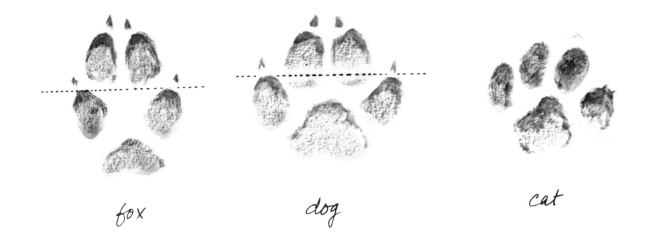

fox   dog   cat

underside
front paw

when you see these whisk marks between the footprints
you are sure that this is not a dog's track...

they come from the tail
that sweeps with every step

the fox eats everything an environment full of small animals has to offer: insects, refuse, eggs, frogs, worms, fruit, plants, berries — everything gets swallowed. Altogether a fox eats about a pound a day. The fox helps rid the environment of sick and weak animals — many a myxomatous rabbit is put out of its misery...

The fox is one of the larger predators.

a digging fox

The fox's den -
often an enlargement
of another animal's
burrow- has four, five or
even more exits -
always handy!

An occasional fox will be so bold
as to go up to the farm at night

this is how the fox
pounces on a mouse

foxes are also
useful:
more than half
of their fare
consists of
mice!

a fox can hear the squeaks of fighting
mice even from a great distance.

the shoulder height
of a fully grown
fox is about 16 inches

the average height of the tunnel
(the entrance to the den)
is about 8 inches

the fox has to squeeze through
like this, often many yards across
and many down

when the weather is good,
a fox likes to take a
short nap in the sun.

Early winter is the foxes' mating time.
You can hear them bark at night.
The dog fox pursues the vixen and
at this time of year you may
encounter them during the day.

Up on his hind legs,
the male circles around his
intended until she responds
to his feelings...

the food deliveries begin almost
as soon as the den becomes home
to the little ones.

if the den is disturbed,
the mother will carry her
pups to a safer place.

as soon as they are big enough
to play outside, the pups with
their adorable scoundrel's faces
like nothing better than to chase
around and tumble.

the fox seldom hunts close
to the den - rabbits may live
right next to a fox hole!

it must be quite maddening for a fox:
on almost all expeditions the hunter
is accompanied by the scolding birds,
so that every rabbit knows he is around.

a fox who abandons his natural
timidity and comes out to bite
people, cattle, or domestic
animals probably
has rabies...

the bite of a rabid fox can
endanger the lives of people
and animals

The Roe Deer

One of the most graceful wild animals is the roe deer. Though I think of my own country when I think of roe deer, these beautiful creatures are found from Scandinavia and Britain through central and southern Europe to the Mediterranean. Two other races, the Siberian and the Manchurian roe deer, inhabit Asia. In recent times, European roe deer have increased in number. Southern England probably has more than ever. In addition, roe deer have been introduced in various parts of North America, where they reside chiefly on large private preserves. In Texas, for example, an outdoorsman accustomed to the sight of whitetailed deer and mule deer, might be startled by the appearance—a very different appearance—of the tailless, short-antlered, small-bodied roe deer.

As woods and open country become noisier because of traffic and recreational activities, roe deer turn into predominantly nocturnal animals. To have a good chance of seeing roe deer, you have to park your car quietly by the roadside and then scan the meadows and fields along the edges of the woods with your binoculars. The best time to look is either in the morning or just when it is getting dark.

Roe deer are ruminants—they are hooved animals who chew a cud. The male is called a buck, the female a doe. A little smaller than the common farm goat, they are much more elegant. During the summer, roe deer are a reddish brown; in winter their fur turns a soft gray. In the late spring the fawns are born. If you find a fawn, you should not come too close. The mother probably is standing not far away, frightened to death by the intrusion. Moreover she knows instinctively that her scent is stronger than the fawn's, and she must keep away from her young while an intruder is near.

The greatest life expectancy for roe deer is about 17 years, but usually by the time they are 11 or 12 years old, their teeth are so worn down that the end is likely to be near.

Roe deer need 8 to 10 pounds of green food a day: cultivated crops in the fields, leaves and twigs of trees and bushes, and in the wintertime buds, acorns, and beechnuts. A roe deer makes very few sounds. Bucks and doe call each other during the mating season with a deep "feep" sound, made through almost completely closed nostrils. The doe and her fawns, too, talk to each other in this way. A suddenly startled roe will emit a "bow, bow" sound after a delay of several minutes. If you did not know any better, you might think it was a dog.

Each roe deer needs about 25 acres of land. Rabbits, hares, pheasants, and so on may share it, but no other deer.

Many deer are hit by cars. When driving through wooded areas one should be very careful, especially early in the morning and at dusk.

Two full-grown males. A roebuck on the left, a red deer on the right.
The roebuck is built so that he can slip and sneak through
dense, bushy cover. The noble red deer
originally lived on the plains.

———————

A roe deer is not a red deer,
a roe is also not a young red deer
and does not turn into a
red deer once grown up.

Just as a pony looks
like a foal — but does not
turn into a horse, even if
the pony lives to be
extremely old!

And just as a goat is not
a small cow, so a roe deer
is not a small red deer.

They belong to the same family,
yet they are different animals.

Footprint of a roe deer walking quietly

When a roe deer is fleeing, the dewclaws also touch the ground, making small indentations behind the prints of the large hoof lobes.

You can find out if any roe deer live in the vicinity, even if you do not actually see them.

You can see their footprints on sand paths and especially on snow-covered ground.

There are also other signs: to mark his territory the buck will leave scratch patches here and there on the ground around tree trunks.

The so-called "buck rubs" on trees indicate that a buck lives nearby. Where bark is missing from the lower parts of trees it usually is peeled off by rabbits.

Where there is cover, quiet, and food, preferably in woods bordered by fields and meadows, there may be roe deer.

But roe deer can thrive in reed fields where there is not a tree in sight.

During the day roe deer mostly
stay hidden, and lie abed -
in a shallow hollow, free of leaves
and prickly twigs. There they sit
dozing and chewing their cud.

as soon as it gets darker,
deer come out to graze
in the fields.

_____

An old, suspicious buck
leaves the thickets only when
it gets almost too dark
to see anything.

Once out of their cover, roe deer are on the alert every moment!
To stay abreast of things, they primarily use their noses to catch the wind. The nose has to be wet. (if you want to feel where the wind is coming from, you hold up a wet finger). Roe deer can smell human scent to a distance of 700 to 1000 feet. Because their eyes are astigmatic they can see moving objects more readily than stationary ones.

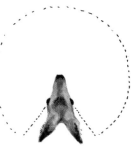

their eyes are set far apart at the sides of the head - they give a wide range of view.

Their hearing is remarkable. Familiar sounds do not frighten them: a train may thunder right by. But the sound of a twig snapping alerts them, and they are ready for flight!

If a deer is disturbed, but not really sure why, he pretends to keep on grazing. He bends his head as if he were feeding, then swiftly lifts his head again, to look into the suspicious corner.

During a storm the roe deer cannot pick up scents very well: the nose is not much use when the air is swirling around. And it is hard on the eyes, too, and the ears are no help when branches are crashing...
roe deer then choose the known over the unknown: they stay in concealing thickets!

The most striking differences between a buck and a doe are, of course, the buck's antlers

"paintbrush" buck

"apron" doe

Buck and doe have different rump patches. These are especially obvious on their winter fur →

the rump patch of a startled, fleeing roe deer is spread out. It then seems twice as big.

roe deer have virtually no tails.

To point out the difference between a young and a full-grown buck, I have put them next to each other here

In reality you would not see this too often: an older buck does not want a young fellow in his territory and above all not during the mating season. An intruding buck does well to keep pretty much under cover!

If he becomes too bold, he risks getting a good beating!

Antlers like these are the most beautiful head gear a buck can have. They are about 5 feet high

It is not true that you can tell the age of an animal from the number of points on his antlers

a roe buck is not
a sweet little
"Bambi"

several times,
I have watched one spear
another to death.

An older, irritable buck whose
antlers have degenerated into
two sharp daggers over the
course of years can mercilessly
play havoc with these weapons!

He can storm toward an
unsuspecting young buck
and because his antlers have
no tines their sharp points are
especially dangerous.

Ordinarily the tines catch on
those of a rival, thereby
preventing a severe goring.

The rutting season of the roe deer
falls in mid-summer.

The panting buck
pursues the doe.

You might see a well-worn
circle around a
freestanding tree or bush,
a so-called roe ring.

a doe and a buck
have chased each other
for hours there.

A buck will repeatedly
mount (cover) a doe as
long as she is in heat.
When she no longer accepts
him, he looks for another.

He has no permanent mate
and later on pays no
attention to his offspring.

newborn
fawn

the fawn weighs about
3 pounds at birth
and begins to nibble
at leaves after
about a week

In late spring the doe has one, often two
fawns. Precious little things! And
how well the good Lord has planned it:
a newborn fawn does not have any
odor during the first days. Dogs,
foxes, and so on can practically
brush by without smelling anything.
When the fawn is 3 or 4 months old
the white spots gradually disappear
and the little buck displays the first
signs of knobs on his forehead.

In 8 or 9 months the first antlers start to grow and they are almost complete by the end of a year

but the velvet still has to be rubbed off.

This is a normal little rack of antlers for a "yearling"

Six months later, the little antlers fall off again... immediately afterward, new and stronger antlers begin to grow.

the same buck

← here in his winter coat with velvet antlers

In his summer → coat with polished antlers

This little buck is called a knob buck because his antlers are still knobby. ↓

a buck with this kind of antlers is called a spike buck ↓

Six-point buck

A fork buck

A real pest for the roe deer is the botfly,
a strange, fat fly that plagues the deer
during the summer months.
It buzzes around a deer's head
and squirts its larvae into the nostrils.
The larvae creep into the air passages.
If the larvae form thick clusters,
the deer practically cannot breathe
anymore, and runs around lean as
a rake, rattling and coughing...

True size

The deer is instinctively aware
of the danger of the botfly
and tries to escape by
shaking his head and
fleeing, but the pest
often wins...

larvae that are coughed
out pupate - turn into
new botflies!

Every year, many animals are
also killed by traffic

The fox will try to grab
a fawn while the doe is
not paying close attention

and when the
wild boar stumbles
upon a fawn, he knows
what to do...

and above all, do not
discount poaching dogs!

In the winter, deer like to run together.
　　Such a herd is called a "bevy," a bevy of roe deer

They live
mainly on buds
from trees and
bushes, and
on beechnuts
and acorns

hind leg of
a roe deer

By marking grass and leaves
with excretions from their glands,
roe deer leave scent tracks.
Scent is very important in the
animal world. It enables
a buck to find a doe.
The scent of a sick animal is
different from that of a healthy
one. Smelling a track, the fox
knows whether it is worthwhile
to follow an animal and
whether he has a sure catch!

occasionally you will find
a black deer.

Roe deer are excellent swimmers,
but if the bank is too steep
they may drown ...

They need a little "step ladder" here and there
where the banks are too steep

The Black Grouse

The shy black grouse, "with an eye on every feather," can only thrive in vast, absolutely undisturbed heath and moorlands. Therefore, unfortunately, there are not too many black grouse.

Not all that long ago, around the turn of the century, there were quite a few. But a lot has changed since then: heath and moorlands have become smaller and are continually getting noisier. Grouse loathe this commotion. They need the heath where there is high heather to breed and newer heather for food. They need birches so that they can feed on the buds in the wintertime. There also have to be some fir trees so that the grouse can shelter from the sun under the low-hanging branches. And above all, peace and quiet.

The male, or blackcock, is as big as a dwarf-cock. His color is beautiful burnished blue-black. He has feathered claws, burning red "roses" above the eyes, and a lyre-shaped tail with a curved sickle on either side. The older the cock, the larger and curvier the sickles. The female, or grayhen, is less spectacular, and for a reason. For a good four weeks she sits on the ground, brooding her clutch. The less visible she is the better. The hen sits very steadily on her eggs and gives off little scent then. From a distance of as little as five feet, a dog with a good nose will not be able to smell her. Like almost all chickenlike birds, black grouse prefer running to flying, though they are good fliers— fast as an arrow.

The blackcock is at his most impressive during the spring mating season. About an hour before sunrise, blackcocks assemble in an open area to wait for the grayhens. The oldest cock has the most hens.

The younger cocks have to stay at the edge of the courting ground and have nothing better to do than to pretend to pick fights with each other. They hiss, wheeze, jump into the air, beat their wings, spin around in circles. You can hear their deep cooing from a distance.

When the grayhens appear at the courting place, the blackcock goes into full swing! With lowered head, tail high with the sickles spread out, wings hanging down next to his feet, the cock circles around the hen. She acts as if she found this behavior absurd. You often observe this in female animals! The performance continues until the sun appears on the horizon. And listen! The moment the sun comes up, instantly there is complete silence! Then the red ball rises above the horizon and there it starts again: a delightful uproar, fluttering, and carrying on. The hen lays seven to eight eggs in a nest in high heather and they hatch a month later. During the first three weeks after birth, the chicks feed on insects and ant eggs. After that they switch to plants.

Thanks to her splendid
protective coloration
the grayhen can hardly
be seen during
breeding season.

The blackcocks appear on the courting
ground before daybreak.
the grayhens come a little later.
Meanwhile the cocks have been
busy with mock fights — they
perform twisted jumps in the air
and run toward each other in
cockfight manner — but they do not
actually attack each other. You hear a
continual "koo-rooh koo-rooh koo-rooh" and
a strange sneezing sound "tchu-shwee" —
a breathtaking display!

the cousin of the black grouse
is the capercaillie
who lives in the woods,
hills, and mountains.

In areas where
they both live,
they interbreed
regularly.

During the winter black grouse
like to roost in birches—
they eat the buds
(in German the blackcock
is called the birchcock)

grouse
chick

The Wild Boar

Wild boars have lairs, or sleeping hollows, in dense pine. Big, old deciduous trees provide them with food: acorns, beechnuts, and chestnuts. They are useful in the forest. While they are looking for food, they completely turn over the upper soil.

Several subspecies of these wild swine (from which domestic hogs were derived long ago) are distributed through most of Europe, Asia, and northern Africa. In 1893 an American sportsman imported some from Germany's Black Forest to stock a hunting preserve in New Hampshire. In 1910 another sportsman released some Russian boars on a hunting preserve in North Carolina near the Tennessee border. There have also been a few subsequent American importations. Today, America's wild boars—or those closest in type to their wild European ancestors—are found chiefly in Tennessee and North Carolina. A great many are found in other states (notably California), where they are the result of hybridization between wild and stray domestic swine. These are equally wild.

Wild boars are intelligent, smarter than most other ungulates, meaning animals with hoofs. They cannot see especially well with their small eyes, but they have extraordinarily sharp ears and noses.

The females form groups. The male prefers to stay by himself. During the rutting season—the winter mating time—the male will join a "sounder," as the herd is sometimes called. Often he has to fight another male for the females. Males attack each other with their formidable tusks; those are not just decorations! The lower tusks are especially dangerous weapons which can be up to ten inches long. In winter a male boar is a block of black, rugged strength. Looking at him, you would not expect this square hulk to be able to gallop at such frightful speed, as fast as a deer! With his wedgelike shape he smashes right through the underbrush . . .

Snow and frost do not affect him very much. Under his black bristles there is a woollen undershirt and his thick skin covers a layer of fat. In a year when there are many acorns and the like, that layer of fat gets to be two or three inches thick. When you encounter the same animal in the summer, you will hardly recognize him. Instead of a black, hairy, thick-set creature you will see a long-legged, brownish gray animal with a long, thin head, looking more like a tapir than a wild boar. In spring, the sow gives birth to from two to twelve pretty striped piglets who are barely visible in the forest, thanks to protective coloring. The sow is a brave and attentive mother.

the powerful canine teeth of the boar
are constantly growing.
they are dangerous
weapons.

By continually
grinding them
against each other,
the boar keeps them
razor sharp

the longer tusks
are set in the lower jaw

the footprints of boar
and red deer resemble
each other somewhat,
but the red deer's track
shows no dewclaws

boar print   red deer

Wild boars are nocturnal creatures

During the day they hide in dense pine forests.
As soon as darkness falls they appear.

While searching for food, the boar
turns over the ground with the
sensitive saucerlike disk at
the end of his snout

This helps form humus
on the forest floor

Boars are omnivorous
and will eat worms,
larvae, young mice,
pupae, acorns,
horse chestnuts,
and beechnuts.

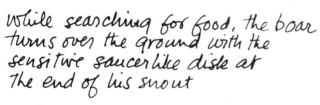

Wild boars will
also eat carrion—
wild animals
that have died.

They can be a real
plague in farm fields!
A great deal may be
trampled down
and eaten.

They can ravage a potato
or wheat field in just one night!

Boars are bothered quite
a bit by external parasites
and so they wallow daily —
they take a mud bath.
Grunting comfortably, the boar
lies down in a wet loam pit
and rolls around, thereby
relieving itching and
removing some of the vermin.
the dried mud — in which
lice, ticks, and fleas are
stuck — gets rubbed off
on a tree.

Wild boars can be dangerous when they have been cornered. Sows who have piglets cannot be trusted.

In winter, the mating season,
the males seek each other out.

During that period
they fight rambunctiously

Boars are not gentle lovers
and the sow screams to high heaven
at times! The gestation period
is about 4 months.

A piglet with his
splendid striped pajamas.
He can hardly be
detected among dry
leaves and ferns.

This little one
already has
sizable teeth

In the spring the sow bears her litter of piglets.
The number varies from 2 to 12.
Woe to whoever gets caught between
the mother and her young!

A piglet of
7 or 8 months.
the pajama
stripes have
disappeared.

occasionally a shaggy
black boar mates with a
domestic sow - he must
see something in a
blond maiden ...

Their children do not
turn out to be
very beautiful   →

A herd of wild boars

the same boar

here in his summer coat

here in his winter fur

During the winter the wild boar is quite a bit more impressive in his heavy bristles.

Two friends who favor
twilight hours and dense cover...
They often live in the same
habitat and use the same trails.

One of the worst enemies of small wild animals: the carrion crow

Our superstitious ancestors heard tidings of death in the dismal croaking of the crow.

Ducks and hares do not have to be superstitious — they instinctively know that their offspring are quite likely to be killed...

And this is how the crow goes about it: first it pecks the eyes out...

Sometimes Destructive Wildlife

The following animals are not particularly harmful to people and cultivated crops but can cause damage in the animal world. This does not happen when they appear in normal numbers—they may be useful then. But as soon as there are too many of them, they cause problems.

The crafty carrion crow is one of the worst offenders. Crows move about quickly, especially in the spring and summer. A mother duck with her brood on the way to the water—a swift dive—one young duckling gone—and another, and another . . . . There are too many crows!

Other evil characters are the magpie and the jay. They, too, know the ropes! I sat and watched once, early in the morning when everybody was still asleep: trip, trip, they walk in the rain gutters, peer under every tile of the roof, and find all the nests. Songbirds are easy victims. In some regions things have become too easy for the crow, magpie, and jay because their natural enemies—the hawk and the falcon—have been gradually disappearing. The dwindling of these birds of prey has been agriculture's gift to the crow family. Besides the members of the crow family, other birds must survive; there has to be a healthy balance.

European Jay

Sitting quietly on the watch,
the jay soon finds out where
that little bird with the
food in its beak is
headed all the time...

A few jays can
kill off most of
the songbirds in
a sizable part
of the forest!

the clever magpie, too, is fond
of eggs and young birds.
Hedges and the sides
of bushes are combed
carefully.

the hooded crow
prefers carrion
and refuse,
and does
little harm.

the European rook,
about as big as
a crow, breeds in
large colonies, but
is not a great pest.

rook ↗

crow
↓

jackdaw
↓

Carnivorous predators
generally hunt during the night,
sleep during the day.

the polecat, about 2 to 2½ feet long, is a large
European species of weasel. He lives in thickets,
hedges, and haystacks; hunts rabbits and young
wild animals; feeds on fruit, insects, fish, and
eggs. Frogs- paralyzed by a bite in the back -
are taken alive and saved for a later snack.
the polecat is useful as a fierce rat catcher.
Under the tail are 2 glands. If cornered, a
polecat can release a horrendous odor!
He is related to the skunk. The European ferret is more
domesticated than the Asian polecat; and paler than the
Western polecat, but akin to both. The North American
black-footed ferret, which preys on prairie dogs, is an
                                        endangered species.

Ermine. about 1 to almost 2 feet long. rabbit, rat, and mouse hunter

the difference between these two: the ermine has a black tail tip.

weasel. about 8 to 10 inches long. found everywhere that the ermine is.

Both these little robbers do a good job cleaning up rats and mice. They are daytime animals, tireless hunters. Something unusual: a female ermine, so young that her eyes are barely open, can already be bred — 8 months later she has her first litter! The weasel wears the same coat in summer and winter. The ermine is snow white in the winter, only the black tail tip remains.

← the weasel lives mainly
on small rodents.

---

the ermine is a fierce little
creature, and will defend
itself against dogs, foxes,
and even people.
rats and rabbits, even
hares (who are 16 times
as heavy as the little
predator) are killed by
a bite on the neck.
During the
rabbit's last
desperate jumps,
the ermine rides its prey
like a horse.

jumps 15 or more
feet in the air!

Red squirrels, too, are counted among harmful
wildlife: they injure softwood and rob nests,
but the red squirrel population has suffered —
a great number have died from a disease about
which biologists still know
very little. So they are not
doing much harm at the
moment... Here and there you
see a pretty red climber.
In a round nest, high up in
a tree, 3 to 6 young are
born. Squirrels often do not
remember where they have
buried their winter supplies,
acorns and beechnuts,
although they can locate
food by its scent.
A lot of stray oaks
have been planted
by squirrels
and jays.

A gnawed-off
pine cone
shows that
a squirrel
sat here,
feeding.

Worse, much worse, than all
    the preceding rascals is
    a cat running wild.
        Less merciful than other wildlife,
        wild cats prowl about killing,
        often purely for fun.

            the young of these wild cats,
            born somewhere in a rabbit hole,
            become noticeably bigger and
            healthier than the average
                house cat.

Poaching dogs, too, especially when
there are two or more of them, soon
masters the chase: one circles around
and rouses the wild animal,
the other waylays it.

an uncommon sight!

badgers only
come out of their
holes at night.

badger fat was
once supposed to
have healing power.

_____

badgers feed on
mice, eggs, worms,
insects, and carrion.

A cousin of the weasel, the otter
has webbed feet for swimming.
But dirty, polluted water! the otter
cannot cope with that...
The closely related American river
otter were depleted at one time
by excessive trapping. In the
United States, they still inhabit
the upper Midwest, and areas of
the Southeast. There, too,
they are menaced by pollution.

The Duck

The problem with mallard drakes is that they are "oversexed." I have often been
very upset watching their merciless male assaults. No female duck is safe when she is
outnumbered by a troop of drakes. The drakes fasten their beaks to the back of the hen
duck's head and push her under water. If she is lucky, she may escape breathlessly
through the waterplants. Quite often, the duck drowns and then her brood will also perish.
You can do little to stop this wretched behavior beyond throwing a stick at the drakes.

What do domesticated animals have to do with the mallards? In some parts of Europe
and America mallards are not wild ducks anymore. Frequently they crossbreed with
barnyard ducks, producing hybrids, and hardly lead a true wild existence. Both the
hybrids and the pure mallards sit on park ponds and canals. They do not have to worry
about food. As soon as the first rays of spring sun appear, mothers arrive with their baby
carriages and bags full of stale bread . . . the ducks eat themselves round and lazy.

When the mother ducks come out with their ducklings after a month, they too swim in
circles, begging. When things were still the way they are supposed to be, the mother ducks
would swim to the banks with their little ones in order to catch mosquitoes and flies.

The natural food for mallards consists of waterplants, insects, worms, and the like. And
last, but not least: cultivated crops! True mallards—who can live to be 18 years old—are
seminocturnal animals. During the day, they sit hidden in thickets and reeds. During the
summer, you may have looked in vain for the handsome, beautifully marked drake with
his blue-green head and curly tail feathers. But at that time of year he looks different—
almost as uniform in color as the female. In the fall, his pretty colors appear again.

The mallard's relation, the wild goose, will not get involved with the tame members of
its family and has remained a true wild bird. Shy and smart, a wild goose can live to be
40 years old! When you are outside in the autumn, watch the sky. These migrating birds
flying south in V-formation are an impressive sight. They tell you that the summer is
definitely over.

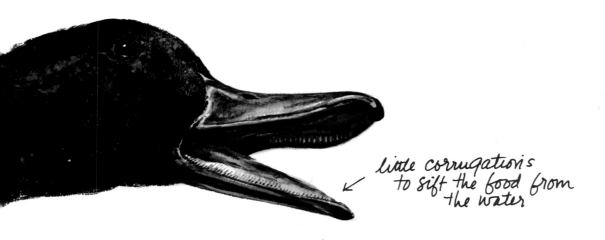

little corrugations
to sift the food from
the water

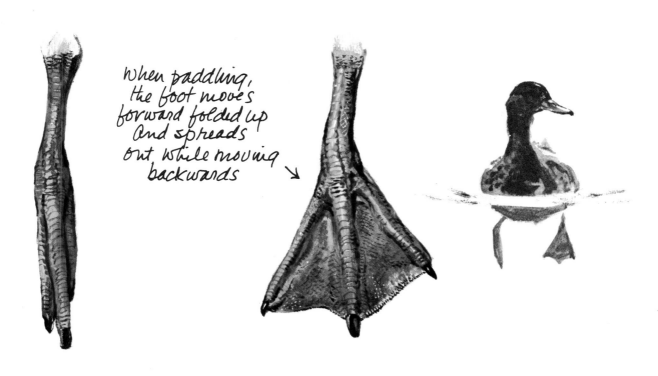

when paddling,
the foot moves
forward folded up
and spreads
out while moving
backwards

Only the mallard drake has
beautiful curled tail feathers.

The hen mallard has just slipped out of her nest and flip — there are the drakes again! First Will, then Jim, then Pete, and then finally Cornelius once again!

Every spring the same hassle.

Many ducks drown during those merciless assaults and their many broods are lost.

Hidden in the thicket
the duck builds her nest
↓

The nest is lined
with down.
The hen lays
8 to 15 eggs.
The duck sits on
them for 4 weeks.

Ducklings, just out of the egg,
do not eat anything during
the first 48 hours. After that, the mother
takes her young to the water
to look for mosquitoes
dancing above the surface.

The mother duck
has to watch closely:
robbers are lurking
everywhere!

One of the
ducklings' worst
enemies is the
pike: many little
ducks disappear
without a sound...
water rats, too,
pull the ducklings
down.
There are duck
fanciers above
water too:

crow, seagull, heron, ermine, cat
and others...

Swaus nesting
nearby are also
dangerous:
they will hold
a duckling under
water till he drowns.
Coots will peck young ducks
to death...

Mallards who crossbreed
with tame ducks
in parks or barnyards
produce ugly hybrids.

Mallards are seminocturnal.
During the day, they find
shelter in thickets and reeds
or on the safe open water.
Toward evening they take wing
and come to forage
on land...

By the hundreds, even thousands,
they land in a wheat field
which they flatten out in order
to nibble the grain.

In one night, they can destroy
a field of barley or peas!

At dawn the mallards
return to their daytime
resting place.

Ducks make their feathers waterproof with oil from their preen gland.

By tipping their heads - or dabbling - they can look for animals and plants underwater.

35-50 miles per hour!

When mating,
the drake holds
onto the back of
the hen's head.

Besides the mallard, there are many other kinds of ducks...

pintail

widgeon

shoveler

tufted duck

eider

pochard

teal

red-crested
pochard

the shelduck,
who breeds in
rabbit holes

Ducks landing in a stubble field

Geese like to feed on grass and grain
↓

Geese graze during the day and sleep at night on open water — exactly the opposite of some ducks.

the protected barnacle goose visits Holland by the thousands during the winter.

this is a European species that occasionally strays across the Atlantic to North America

the greylag goose.
ancestor of our
domestic goose.
wingspread 5 feet.
very intelligent
animals with
extremely sharp eyes.

rabbit

hare

The Hare and the Rabbit

To show the visible difference between a hare and a rabbit as clearly as possible, I have drawn their portraits together on one page.

Let us begin with the bigger one: the hare, a familiar character in legends and tales. In *Reynard, the Fox* he is called Cuwaert and to me that sounds like the English word "coward." But that is really not quite fair; as an animal who lives on flat land and has no burrow like the rabbit's, he cannot do much besides run or crouch. Often you can see by his looks that he does not know which strategy to choose.

Older hares are very susceptible to a variety of parasites like the liver fluke. Four times a year, the female produces a litter of two to four young. A pregnant female can be bred again before giving birth and then has two litters inside her at the same time!

But for ambitious multiplication work we rely on rabbits. Four to seven times a year a doe produces a litter of four to nine. The first litter becomes sexually mature that same year. Here and there real population explosions occur, and where rabbits are numerous they can be destructive. America's rabbits are various subspecies of cottontails, which do not dig burrows as the European species does, but seek to escape from cold or predators in the burrow of some other animal. In a few regions European rabbits have also been introduced. America has hares, too—the varying, or snowshoe, hare and the arctic hare, which are quite similar to one of the European hares—as well as jack rabbits, which are really hares. Rabbits and hares are plentiful in America, but cause no serious agricultural problem because they are kept in check by hunting.

The wild rabbit is about as big as the domestic dwarf variety and a good deal smaller than the hare. The rabbit has a pretty, soft, gray fur and a pleasantly rounded outline like a cuddly bedtime toy. The rabbit's eyes are dark, the hare's are lighter. The rabbit is a short-distance sprinter.

the hare, like the typical long-distance runner, has long legs.
Wearing a salt-and-pepper colored, rougher coat, the hare sleeps
outside in all kinds of weather, while the rabbit sits cozily inside.

Seen from the back, the upright little white tail distinguishes the rabbit. The hare holds his tail down most of the time. The upper side of the tail is black, and the tips of the ears, too.

the difference in size can clearly be seen this way
↓

the hare likes to be alone

the rabbit is gregarious
and lives in a group.
the strongest buck is the boss
and has the best does.

The hare has no burrow.
His sleeping place is
a shallow depression
in the grass or brush,
where he spends almost
all day in a so-called
form or squat.

The hare uses several
definite forms, depending
on the wind direction.
North American rabbits,
cottontails, behave more
like hares. They, too,
rest or hide in forms.

a disturbed
crouching hare.
flatter and
flatter...
till the hare
resembles a
molehill.

An experienced hare distinguishes
sounds and does not run away
from the familiar clattering of
the farm wagon - just crouches.
But if anything suspicious does
come too close, he darts out
of the form and disappears
hastily, at top speed!
Later, when the danger is gone,
the hare comes back via
a long detour.

the incisors, which
are always growing,
are ground off against
each other. If one breaks
off. the opposite one
keeps growing.
Within a few weeks
it will grow into
the other jaw and
the hare will starve.

———

to reconnoiter,
the hare stands on
his hind legs.

———

When caught,
a hare will scream,
and sounds like
a crying baby.

Around the beginning of each year,
the hares' mating time starts.
Six weeks later, the newborn leverets
drop from their mother's warm body
into the icy winter weather...
　　　　　　　　　and not one of them has a
　　　　　　　　　burrow or anything like it...

How a cow can ever catch a hare, I have no idea,
but occasionally you see young cattle chase
after a hare – who isn't in much danger...

the hare's real enemies
are the black crow
and the poaching cat,
who are both especially
fond of young hares.

rain and humidity bother
the hare a great deal –
then the liver fluke soon appears

A newborn hare comes into the world fully equipped.

Little rabbits
are not quite
"finished" yet,
and still
require several
weeks in the nest
to get ready.

after 14 days
their eyes are open
and they have some fur.

Rabbits prefer to live in
sandy areas - they can dig
holes there. If they live on clay
ground, where they cannot dig,
they will make their homes in a
trench under some low branches.

Often the burrows of many rabbits will form a big system of tunnels called a warren...
the chambers and corridors are all connected and everywhere there are escape tunnels leading upward.

practically
everything
green is
considered food!

Rabbits can
seriously damage
fields and forests.

During the winter
the rabbit peels bark
from trees —
orchards can easily
be destroyed this way.

Before giving
birth, the doe digs
a separate hole,
the nesting stop,
which she lines
with fur and
grass. Twice
every 24 hours
the mother comes
to nurse her young.

She scratches
the closed
← nursery open

When she leaves
again, she covers
up the nest and
← smoothes it over.

When there is a
severe frost at
night, the covered
and flattened
entrance may
become so hard
that the mother
cannot get in ...
the first litter sometimes
perishes this way.

25 miles per hour!

the rabbit can swerve
and zigzag extremely well!

On his hind legs
a rabbit looks
over the plain.

To warn the family of possible danger,
the rabbit drums violently on
the ground with hind legs—
instantly, little heads pop up
everywhere, and in moments
everyone is underground.

When the myxoma virus infects a rabbit, it usually dies
after swaying around for a while with an ulcer-infected head.
The poor myxomatous wretch is a pitiful sight...
Fortunately, the disease is not a problem in North America.

I think there
must have been
hundreds of fleas
on this animal!
actually, that is
something that
you see all the
time: if there is
something wrong
with an animal,
it will almost always
be crawling with
parasites.

Occasionally you will see
pitch black rabbits.

Hares and rabbits do not get involved
with each other. There is no crossbreeding,
but there is interbreeding between
domestic and wild rabbits.

The Red Deer

It stands to reason that a rabbit can make himself invisible—even that a roe deer can hide among ferns. But that huge creatures like red deer can find cover! Nor can I understand how they are able to move through dense woods with their big, heavy antlers. But they manage: in big open forests they would be easily visible and they do not like that. So they remain among fir trees during the day. At night, when the tourists, hikers, bicyclists, and riders are gone, the forest belongs to the wildlife. At daybreak they return to their hiding places.

The North American elk, or wapiti, was once considered by some biologists to be the same species as Europe's red deer. Most biologists now classify it as a distinct but very closely related species. If the American and European herds were able to mingle, they could interbreed. At one time wapiti roamed over most of what is now lower Canada and the United States. The spread of human settlements, and particularly agriculture, drove the herds up into heavily forested mountain areas. Today the greatest numbers are found in the Rocky Mountain region, although elk have been reestablished in other widely separated regions. Originally, the name "elk" referred to the European moose, which belongs to the same species as the American moose. Among all the true deer only the moose is larger than the wapiti. The name "wapiti" is a Shawnee Indian word for pale deer. In the American branch of the family old males tend to be a bleached beige color, considerably lighter than Europe's red deer.

Above all, next to food red deer need quiet and space, and there is not too much of either around. They do not like to be crowded and need a lot of living space. They can starve with stomachs full of nutritionally inadequate food. Especially after a snowfall food is scarce.

During the summer, the stag is reddish brown. His winter coat is grayish brown. The stag lives as long as 15 years. Between 10 and 14 years of age he sets his most magnificent antlers. Every year the antlers are shed and new ones grow. He needs calcium in his food for new antlers. A sick stag grows a poor rack. If a stag has an accident to his right hind leg or hind quarter, the left beam of his rack will be noticeably smaller than the right one.

As in the case of roe deer, the number of points on the antlers does not indicate the animal's age.

In their daytime cover red deer doze and chew their cud. During any twenty-four-hour interval they sleep for only a few hours, and never so deeply that they fail to be roused by the audible approach of what could be an enemy. In America male wapiti are called bulls and the females are called cows, while in Europe a male red deer is called a stag and a female is a hind.

Before the rutting season begins in the fall, the stags become as idle as nature permits. For weeks they eat themselves round and fat, so that they can begin mating when they are as fit as possible. Before and after the rutting season males and females live apart. A group of hinds follows a leader. A company of stags will send a young stag ahead—clever!—to see if the coast is clear. An old, suspicious stag may live by himself with only one young lookout assistant.

In addition to red deer I will picture the much smaller fallow deer—not as small as a roe deer but far from the size of a red stag. It is a distinct species that cannot interbreed with either the roe or the red deer. The name fallow refers to its most common winter color—a kind of pale, sandy yellow. But this is misleading because it exhibits more color variations—black, white, cream, silver-gray, and so on—than any other wild animal. In summer this deer usually becomes dappled with white spots like a fawn. The species originally inhabited the Mediterranean region and small areas of Asia. In those parts of the world wild fallow deer still exist. But the animals easily become almost tame, and they have been established as park deer throughout most of Europe. In recent years they have also come to America, both as park deer and—on large preserves in wild regions—as exotic game animals. Although fallow deer feel at home in children's parks (in contrast to red deer) they also fare splendidly in the wild.

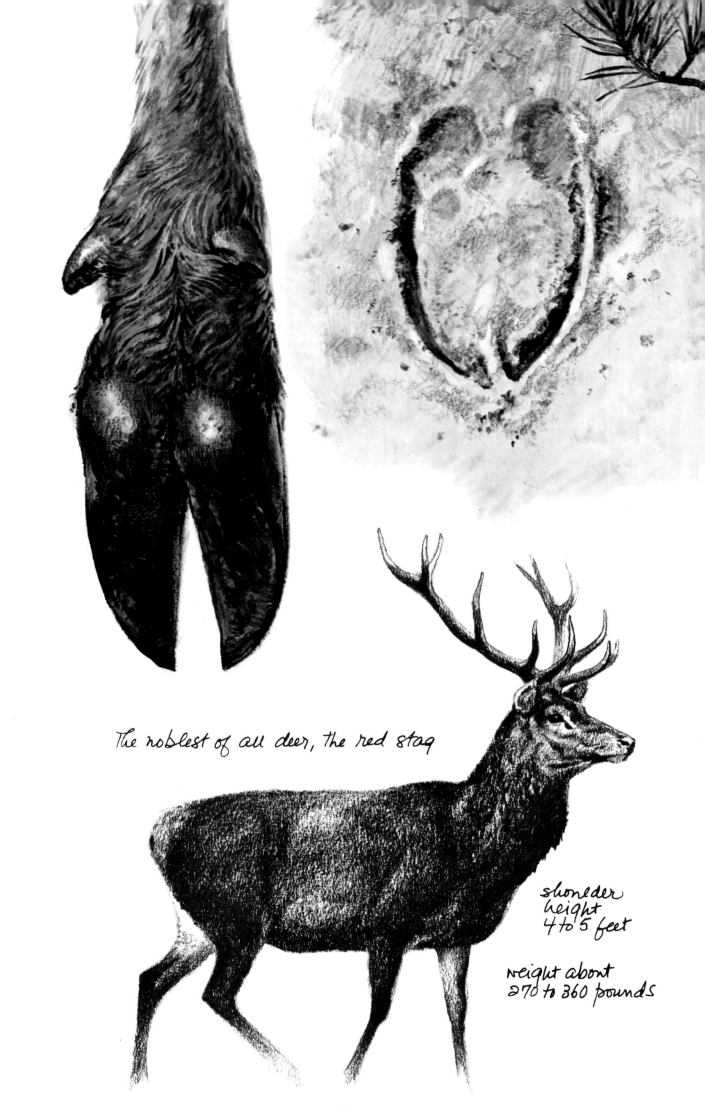

The noblest of all deer, the red stag

shoulder
height
4 to 5 feet

weight about
270 to 360 pounds

deer lice —
hundreds infest
a deer's fur

Portrait of a hind,
a little smaller than the stag,
about 160 to 200 pounds.

An unusual remnant from
ancient times: full-grown
red deer have canine teeth
in their upper jaws, so-called
"vestigial canines." Like other
deer they lack upper incisors.

During the rutting season, the stag "bugles" — an impressive high-pitched sound that can be heard from far away.

Breeding occurs in early autumn

Before and after the rutting season
    males and females live apart.

            at top, a company of stags
            below, a group of hinds

Two equally strong stags
must fight for the harem
and exhausting battles
take place.

Younger stags do not
let it come to that:
as soon as the ruling stag
appears they scamper off...

During the rutting season
the stag is constantly
on guard - he has
no time to feed.
After the mating period
he looks scrawny,
worn out.

velvet
antlers

occasionally,
a stag will be stabbed
to death by his rival.

When antlers are still covered with velvet,
the front hoofs are used for fighting

From a safe distance,
a young stag looks longingly
at the harem. While the ruling
stag drives away another intruder,
the young stag will attempt to steal
one of the females — the ruling stag
chases back and forth...

in early summer the fawn is born
in a well-hidden spot.

young stag

older stag

staqs don't bother
    to look "Youthful at any cost"
        as they qet older

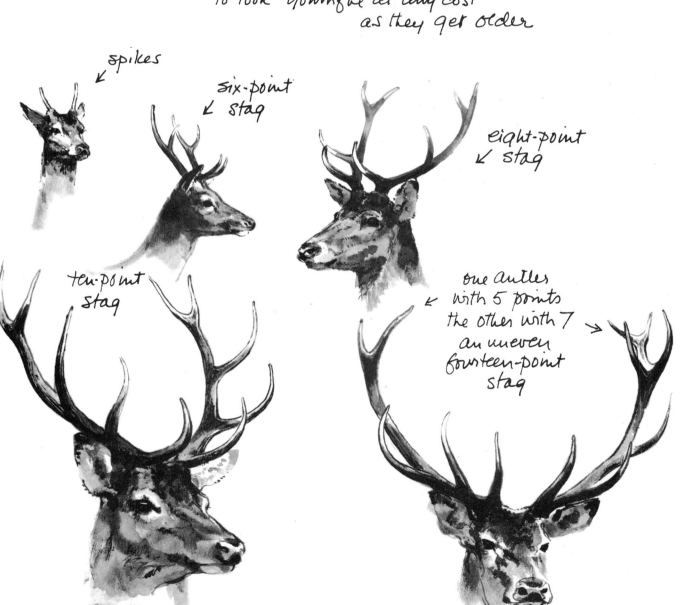

spikes

six-point
stag

eight-point
stag

ten-point
stag

one antler
with 5 points
the others with 7
an uneven
fourteen-point
stag

in the winter, the stag sheds his antlers

Two weeks later there are already new velvet knobs ↓

by the middle of summer, the velvet antlers are ready, then have to be rubbed clean

the velvet is rubbed off against trees

polished in late summer, a rack weighs 11 to 20 pounds

crown

tres-tine

beam

bez-tine

brow tine

base

Sometimes red deer live in areas
where there is not enough natural food.
In some remote, quiet woodlands,
feeding stations have been set up
and are refilled every day.

Fallow deer.
shoulder height 32 to 44 inches.
weight 130 to 200 pounds.
They originated in Asia Minor
and the Mediterranean.
Fallow deer have palmated antlers
and are chestnut red with light spots.
There are also some sepia-colored
animals. They live mostly
in zoos and parks. Sometimes
escaped park animals
live in the wild.

Fleeing fallow deer
have a peculiar way
of bounding – they
leap along with all
4 legs off the ground
at once.

A 3-year-old fallow buck
(the darker variety)
with crippled
antlers

In the deer
family, only
males have antlers.
This is not the case
with reindeer
or caribou.

a yearling fallow
buck with his first
velvet antlers

Ruminants,
as you can
see in this
fallow doe,
have no
teeth →
in their
upper
jaws.

A fallow deer
5 months
before birth
True size.
Even the hoofs
are formed!

To show the difference:
3 full-grown animals
at left, a roe buck
in the middle, a fallow buck
at right, a red stag

The
Pheasant
and the
Partridge

The almost wanton, colorful splendor of the male pheasant seems appropriate to his Asiatic origins. Today pheasants prefer to live where there are woods, shrubs, or reeds where they can hide, next to farmland where they can find food. They may be something of a pest in freshly sown fields. They are fine fliers. They nest on the ground amid dry grass, grain, or even tall stubble. They love to nest in alfalfa hay. Once in a while, a lazy hen deposits her eggs in another hen's nest, so that there are twenty-five or thirty eggs lying together. Nothing will hatch unless half the eggs are taken out and put into an incubator. Eggs from nests disturbed by mowing or predators can be incubated also. When the chicks have hatched and grown big enough, they are set free.

The males are intelligent and domineering and want several mates. With a crowing call—"kok-kok"—followed by a whirr of beating wings, a male advises other males to keep their distance. Males often fight fiercely, using their spurs, which are fairly long and sharp on older males.

The partridge is another chickenlike bird that lives on insects and weed seeds. Unfortunately, sandy paths where partridges like to take sand baths in order to get rid of parasites are being covered with asphalt, making life more difficult for these birds.

Partridges are gregarious; they live in groups called coveys. Males and females are very particular in their choice of mates. Once a couple have found each other, they are faithful. The male even helps with the rearing of the young, and if anything should happen to the female, he will take over completely, while the male pheasant does not take part at all once mating is over. Young partridges are very vulnerable: if the weather is rainy and cold a lot of them may be lost. Heavy rain in early summer means a poor year for partridges.

There are many kinds of partridges. What I am describing here is the common bird known as the gray partridge—a name that hardly does justice to its beautiful coloration: soft gray, chestnut, and cinnamon. Five subspecies are indigenous to Europe and Asia as far east as central Siberia. In Canada and the United States these birds are known as the Hungarian partridge, because the first ones brought to North America—at about the turn of the century—came from the plains of Hungary. Since that time they have established thriving populations in the farmlands and prairies of many North American regions.

older male

spur of a young male pheasant

Where there is food,
water, and cover,
pheasants can be found:
especially around farms,
where they can eat
crop seeds, weed seeds,
beetles, spiders, larvae,
and fresh greens.

They can be somewhat
harmful, but they also do
useful work. For example,
they are the best means
of controlling the
Colorado potato beetle.

At night they sometimes
roost in a tree.

pheasants are chicken like birds,
runners. But they can also
fly exceedingly well —
a good 50 to 55 miles per hour!

Yet, when in danger,
they first try to steal away
on the ground.

pheasants also crouch.
In a snow-covered field
they remain quite visible,
but if they flatten out
in a furrow or among
dry leaves, they can
hardly be seen...
especially the female
with her protective
coloring.

———

a crouching male

showing off as best he can,
the pugnacious male surveys
his territory at daybreak,
crowing and flapping his wings.

if necessary, there
will be fierce fighting

The female is not a particularly good mother.
she defends her young courageously,
but she cannot count: she sometimes fails
to notice when one of her chicks stays behind ...

During the winter,
the males like to stay
by themselves

Gray partridges usually fly
only short distances

a covey of partridges

the partridge
often takes a bath
in sand or dust.
to shed parasites.

The male is constantly
on watch.

Hedgehogs occasionally
try to steal an egg!

A female partridge
usually lays about
15 eggs

_____

partridges need
the farmer

partridge
chick

The Mouflon

The mouflon, wild sheep originally from Sardinia and Corsica, are hardy, strong animals that live in herds, are rather shy, and have excellent eyesight. A few are always standing guard—you cannot get near them. At ten or eleven years of age, the ram has reached his peak. Crossbreeding with tame sheep is possible, but such hybrids are not welcome, for they are especially destructive tree peelers.

red stags, fallow and roe bucks have antlers, massive beams that are shed every year. these are *not* horns. Cattle, sheep, and goats have horns. They are not shed and grow continuously.

mouflon skull

A horn is hollow and is tightly fastened over a center core.

shoulder height about 28 inches weight about 80 pounds

saddle spot

Sometimes the horns
curve abnormally
and grow into the
unfortunate ram's neck.

Occasionally a ewe
has tiny horns.
The females of other
sheep species also
grow small horns.

In the rutting season
the males ram each other...
You can hear the rumbling
from far off.

ewe
with lamb

a

b

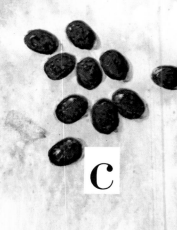
c

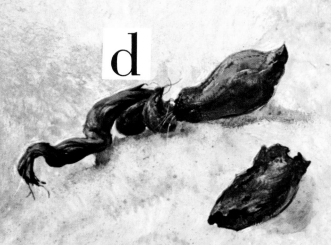
d

e

g

f

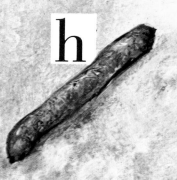
h

different kinds of droppings

a. red deer   b. roe deer
c. rabbit   d. fox
e. hare   f. pheasant
g. goose   h. wild boar

Here is a good idea: start a collection of animal tracks! This is fun for children on vacation. It is quite easy: take any plastic or cardboard box and cut out the bottom, so that only the four sides are left. Place this frame around a footprint and press it into the ground carefully —without damaging the footprint—and your simple casting mold is ready. Take along some powdered plaster of Paris—you can buy it at a paint or hardware store—and mix it with clean water in a small container until it is thick enough to pour. Fill the mold carefully to the rim with this mixture, let it harden (plaster of Paris does not take long), and then remove the frame carefully. Beautiful! Let's find another footprint!